THE LIFE AND TEACHINGS

OF

THE BUDDHA

AN INTRODUCTORY SUTTA STUDY GUIDE

Sacramento Insight Meditation

Jeff Hardin

Sati Press

© Jeff Hardin 2014, third edition
2012, second edition
2010, first edition

This booklet was prepared for a Sacramento Insight Meditation daylong class on An Introduction to *Sutta* Studies offered on January 25, 2014. It is provided for free distribution and not intended for commercial usage. All or part of it may be reproduced without permission from the author provided it is offered free of charge. A digital version of this book is available for free at the Sati Center website. Additional printed copies may be purchased for printing and shipping costs from amazon.com.

The *sutta* passages are quoted from the Access to Insight website (http://www.accesstoinsight.org), John Bullitt, ed., 7/13/2012. The *sutta* translations are those of Ven. Thanissaro Bhikkhu unless otherwise noted. The *Dhammapada* passages are from Gil Fronsdal's translation. *Pāli* terms are used (with Sanskrit variations in parentheses). The Sanskrit version is used for some terms which have become standardized in English such as Dharma, Karma, etc. I am solely responsible for any errors.

The audio files from the *sutta* study daylong are available on the Sacramento Insight Meditation website: www.sactoinsight.org.

Please address inquiries about this book to the author at jeffsimclass@gmail.com.

Table of Contents

Introduction 3
    Why study the *suttas*? 5
    Historical Background 8
    Figure 1. Map of Ancient India at the time of the Buddha. 9
    The *Pāli* Canon 12
    Figure 2. Aśoka Rock Inscription 13
    Figure 3. Outline of the *Tipiṭaka* 15

The Buddha 21
    The Legend of the Buddha 24
    The Quest for Enlightenment 27
    The Decision to Teach the Dharma 35

The Dharma 41
    The First Discourse 41
    Figure 4. *Dhammacakka* 48
    The Second Discourse 51

The *Saṅgha* 55
    The Noble Eightfold Path 57
    Other Important Teachings 61
    Karma and Rebirth 62
    The Four Establishments of Mindfulness 65
    Dependent Origination 67
    The Buddha's Death 73

Conclusion 77

The *Karaṇīya Metta Sutta*	79
Abbreviations	81
Pāli Glossary	83
Acknowledgements	85
References	87

Atha kho bhagavā āyasmantaṃ ānandaṃ āmantesi. Siyā kho panānanda tumhākaṃ evamassa, atītasatthukaṃ pāvacanaṃ, natthi no satthāti. Na kho panetaṃ ānanda evaṃ daṭṭhabbaṃ. Yo kho ānanda mayā dhammo ca vinayo ca desito paññatto so vo mamaccayena satthā ti.

[From his deathbed] ...the Blessed One said to Ven. Ananda, "Now, if it occurs to any of you — 'The teaching has lost its authority; we are without a Teacher' — do not view it in that way. Whatever Dhamma & Vinaya I have pointed out & formulated for you, that will be your Teacher when I am gone.

-From the Mahaparinibbāna Sutta (DN 16.6)

Introduction

Doing no evil,
Engaging in what's skillful,
And purifying one's mind:
This is the teaching of the buddhas.

-Dhp 183.

This booklet gives an introduction to the life and some of the key teachings of the Buddha as they are found by studying the *Pāli Canon*. The Canon is a collection of work that is considered by many Buddhists to be the most complete and accurate representation of what the Buddha and his disciples taught. This present volume, prepared as a study guide companion for a *sutta* study daylong class, bases its representation of the Buddha's teachings on the *suttas*, which are a major part of the *Pāli* Canon. It is not meant as a comprehensive exploration of the Dharma (*Dhamma* in *Pāli*. The term for the Buddha's teachings) or a scholarly exposition of the *suttas*, but as a general introduction. It is my hope that it will serve to inspire the reader to undertake his or her own investigation of the *suttas* with the aid of some of the myriad of study materials and teachers available. Ultimately, it is my wish that the study of these teachings be not solely an academic exercise, but rather that they be investigated, reflected upon, meditated with and put into practice within one's life with the intention of assisting all living beings to awaken to a life free from suffering.

Sutta (*sūtra* in Sanskrit) literally means a thread or line and implies that which holds things together (i.e. similar to English suture). At some point this term also came to mean text and was applied to the early discourses of the Buddha which are existent today in the *Pāli* Canon of the *Theravāda* school of Buddhism. There are many Mahāyāna *sūtras* which are considered by many to be later texts compiled after the time of the Buddha. A more general term for early Buddhist text is *Āgama.* This term includes the *Pāli suttas* and the existing discourse from other non-*Theravāda* schools such as the *Sarvāstivāda* which are found in Sanskrit fragments and Chinese translation.

Undertaking *sutta* study is comparable to traveling to a foreign country in order to discover and learn about another civilization. It can be seen as similar to traveling through space and time to

Ancient India in the days of the Buddha. In order to understand the teachings, we must delve into the thought world of early Buddhism which is spoken in a foreign language – *Pāli*. Although most of the *suttas* are available in English translation and this guide focuses on translated *suttas*, it is still helpful to learn some *Pāli* in order to penetrate the meaning of the *suttas* more deeply. Even in translation, many *suttas* contain ideas and terms that may be unfamiliar and confusing. Here we will encounter gods, demons, saints and realms of existence that seem mythical and far-fetched. There is also a portrait of the human mind and behavior that is straight-forward but profound represented in the *suttas*. The teachings are not meant to be, however, a philosophy or set of theories, but are to be studied, investigated, accepted or rejected, and then put into action.

Why study the *suttas*?

Before embarking on this exploration it is helpful to reflect on the potential motivations for *sutta* study. For many Buddhists throughout the ages the *suttas* have been a rich source of information about the Dharma:

- They describe in detail, from several different perspectives, and with many real-life contexts, how to apply

Dharma practice to our lives. There are numerous examples of skillful and unskillful practice.

- We also get a surprisingly sophisticated explanation of the psychological underpinnings of the human mind with insights and practical advice about how to work with our own.
- Often the *suttas* give us a rich narrative of the Buddha's life and that of his main disciples.
- The Buddha, as a person portrayed in the *suttas*, can be a source of inspiration for us and an example of what is possible in a human life.
- We see a curious and at times provocative view of ancient India, its diverse population, and the religious sects that were rivals of the early Buddhists.
- We can use the Dharma as presented in the *suttas* as a point of reference for other Dharma teachings we may encounter.
- Over time, sutta study can strengthen one's faith in the Dharma as a practical solution to one's difficulties.

In one *sutta* (The *Alagaddūpama Sutta*) the Buddha admonished his followers not to use the teachings to impress others or to win debates. He does this by using one of the many colorful similes found in the *suttas* that further demonstrate the meaning of his words. Here, one who grasps and uses the Dharma incorrectly is compared to one who grabs a poisonous snake by its tail or body and gets bitten by the snake. Whereas one who grabs the snake correctly (e.g. behind its head) does not get bitten and can manage the snake safely: "Their right grasp of those Dhammas will lead to their long-term welfare & happiness." (MN 22) Other caveats or potential pitfalls of *sutta* study include making the study a pure intellectual pursuit and not putting into practice the wisdom gained. Also, some modern readers of the *suttas* carry baggage from prior exposure to religious writings and are triggered into reacting negatively to the *suttas*. This can lead to a closed mind or limit one's potential for being informed or inspired by the *suttas*. Lastly, many of the *suttas* were initially given to a monastic audience and contain advice that is strict, advocating celibacy, a life of renunciation from the pursuit of sensual pleasures and worldly things and ardent spiritual practice. Some *suttas* seem critical or even disparaging of women. The Buddha gave the majority of his teachings to men. Many modern readers find these aspects of the *suttas* stark, uninteresting, irrelevant or even off-putting. If this is the case for you, see if you can read the *suttas*, noticing any resistance that arises for you, hold the teachings as open questions and work with them for some time to see what you can learn from them. They may surprise you and allow you to deepen your practice and to see your defilements more clearly in order to release them and be freer.

Historical Background

The historical backdrop for the Buddha's life and teaching of the Dharma is the Ganges River Basin in ancient India around 500 BCE (see Figure 2). Since this was a preliterate society most of what we know about the Buddha, his teachings, and this period of time comes through the oral transmission of Buddhist teachings. Discourses (*suttas*) spoken by the Buddha were memorized by his followers and continually recited. This was an enormous undertaking given the voluminous amount of teachings from the Buddha and his disciples. The memorized teachings were passed orally from one generation to the next. After about 300-400 years they were subsequently written down and survive in both oral and written forms to this date.

Ancient India at the time of the Buddha was an Iron Age agrarian, feudal society. An economy of surplus allowed for the development of complex social systems which included politics, diplomacy, militarism, and religion. The region was ruled by several kingdoms that exerted control over and eventually subsumed smaller republic states. There was aristocratic intermarriage, constant warfare, diplomacy, trade, and frequent and violent intrigue between the various ruling factions. A social class system, the rudiments of what later became the Indian caste system, was

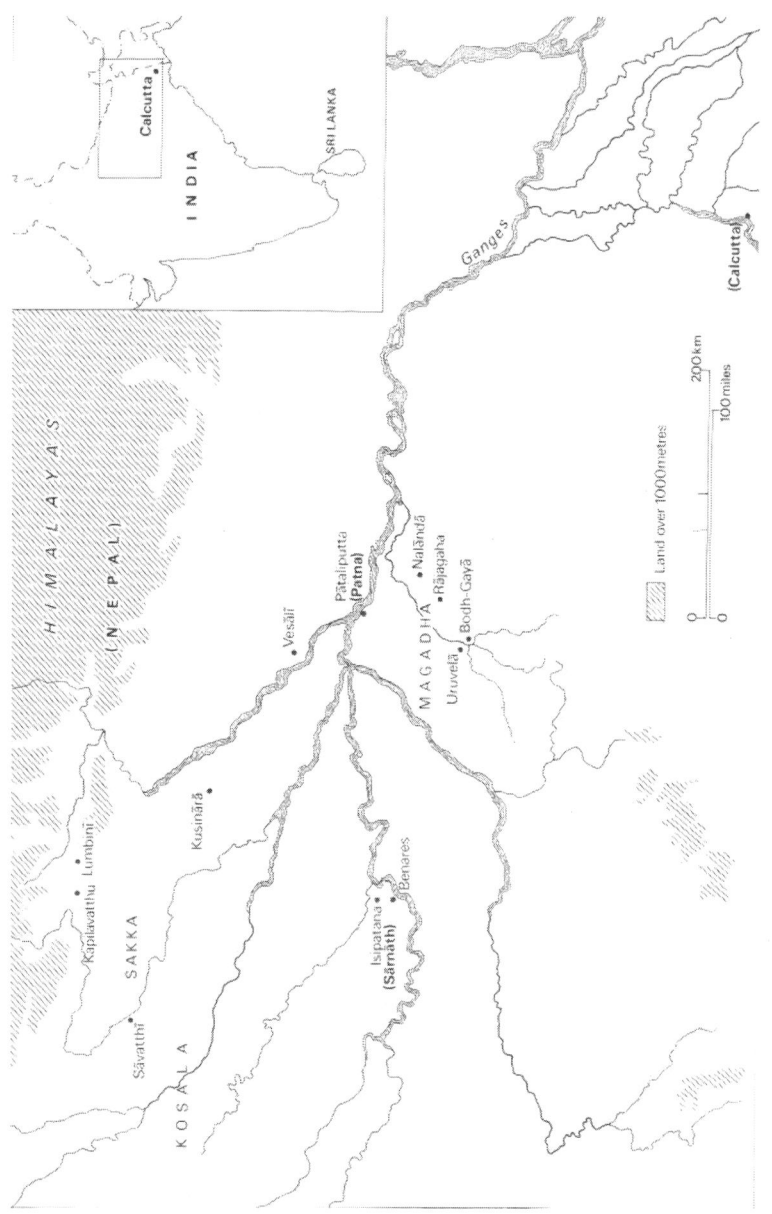

Figure 1. Map of Ancient India at the time of the Buddha.

in place with the *Brahmin* men being regarded as the masters of religious ceremony and hence the highest class. The *Khattiyas* were the rulers and warriors. The *Vessas* were a middle class of merchants and farmers. The *Suddas* were the servants, peasants, and laborers. The lowest ranking citizens were outside of the class system.

There were two main religious groups: the *Brahmins* and the *Samaṇas*. The *Brahmins* were the keepers of the religious tradition of the Vedas. These are ancient hymns that were transmitted orally for millennia and preceded Buddhism by over 1000 year. At the time of the Buddha some of the *Upaniṣads* were known and were popular among the *Brahmins*. The *Upaniṣads* revolutionized ancient Indian thought by developing themes such as the *Brahman* and the *Atman*, or Universal and Individual Selves, *karma* (kamma in *Pāli*), and reincarnation (which differs from the Buddhist concept of rebirth). The *Brahmins* enjoyed prestige and profit from providing religious rituals for those who could pay. The rituals were often sacrifices of materials or animals to appease one or another of the pantheon of Indian gods. This was done both to garner favors for this current life and to be reborn under better circumstances in the next life. The *Brahmins* often owned property and some were wealthy. Brahmanism evolved into what today is the religion of Hinduism.

The *Samaṇas* were a group of wandering truth seekers that arose in reaction to the conservative and often exploitative ranks of the *Brahmins*. Quite a few disaffected men (and some women), many of whom were young *Brahmins*, left their families, jobs, and homes to lead a life in search of spiritual truth. They subsisted by begging for alms food and were mostly respected and supported by the rest of the population. They wandered from town to town and from one spiritual teacher to another. Some practiced forms of meditation, ascetic austerities, fasting, self-mutilation, and celibacy. They would often gather to debate various popular philosophies and religious views. The *Samaṇas* were often resented, ridiculed, and occasionally persecuted by the *Brahmins* whose authority they rejected or undermined.

Surviving Buddhist texts, especially the *Pāli* Canon vividly portrays the conditions of life during the Buddha's day. Existence was harsh, with most of the population engaged in long hours of hard labor. There was frequent warfare, poverty, famine, disease, crime, slavery, corporal and capital punishment (often times doled out capriciously), class exploitation, and for many, an early unpleasant death. Women had an inferior position in society with few, if any, legal rights, and were often treated abusively. Most people during this time, perhaps analogous to our time, were preoccupied with finding ways to minimize the pain and suffering of life while optimizing their enjoyment of sensual pleasures. Making merit by being good and supporting holy men in this life for a better next life was (and still is) common in India.

The *Pāli* Canon

Our current knowledge of what the Buddha taught comes to us from a number of different texts that have been passed from one generation to the next over the last 2500 years. The original words of the Buddha were recorded and repeated in an oral tradition for several hundred years. Around 100 BCE the teachings were written down in India and Sri Lanka. Over time there have been several schisms in the *Saṅgha* (community of Buddhist followers) and the rise of several different Buddhist schools, each with their own version of the original teachings of the Buddha. Additional information comes to us through epigraphic material such as the Asokan rock edicts and pillars which have *Pāli* written in Brahmi script (see Figure 2). These artifacts were generated approximately 200 years after the Buddha's death and contain details of the times including some *suttas*, the names of important monks and significant events in the *Saṅgha* (i.e. councils and schisms).

The *Theravāda* school of Buddhism is considered by many to have a complete and faithful representation of the Buddha's original

Figure 2. Aśoka Rock Inscription in *Brāhmī* Script.

Dharma. Many of the texts from the other schools have been lost or survive in fragmented form. The *Pāli* Canon represents the *Theravāda* collection of the early Buddhist teachings. The language of this Canon is *Pāli* which is believed to be close to the language that the Buddha spoke (probably an idiom called *Magadhi* or perhaps he spoke several idioms spoken in the region). These so called Prakrits existed initially only in oral form but later they were phonetically transcribed into a number of scripts (see page 1 for an example of *Pāli* in roman script). The *Pāli* Canon is also known as the *Tipiṭaka*, which means 'Three Baskets" representing the number of different sections in the Canon (see

Figure 3). The first basket of the *Tipiṭaka* is the *Vinaya-piṭaka* which is the record of the rules given by the Buddha for the proper conduct of monks and nuns and the governance of the original *Saṅgha*. This section also contains many stories explaining the location and circumstances for the formation of each rule. This provides some historical information about the Buddha, his life, and the evolution of the *Saṅgha*.

The second basket is the *Sutta-piṭaka* which is the collection of the numerous discourses spoken by the Buddha and his main disciples. These *suttas* also contain some historical background of the Buddha's life, the early *Saṅgha*, ancient Indian life, and rival sects. This section of the *Pāli* Canon has been of prime importance for most Buddhist practitioners throughout time. In it the details of the Dharma are given. There are general outlines of practice, numerous expositions on specific aspects of the Dharma, depictions of skillful practice contrasted against unskillful practice, and many examples of how the Buddha applied the Dharma to his life or advised others to act in particular circumstances. Generations of meditation practitioners from around the world have used these words to inspire them and guide their meditation practice.

The final section of the *Tipiṭaka* is the *Abhidhamma-piṭaka*. This is a systematic and complex compilation of the Dharma that serves

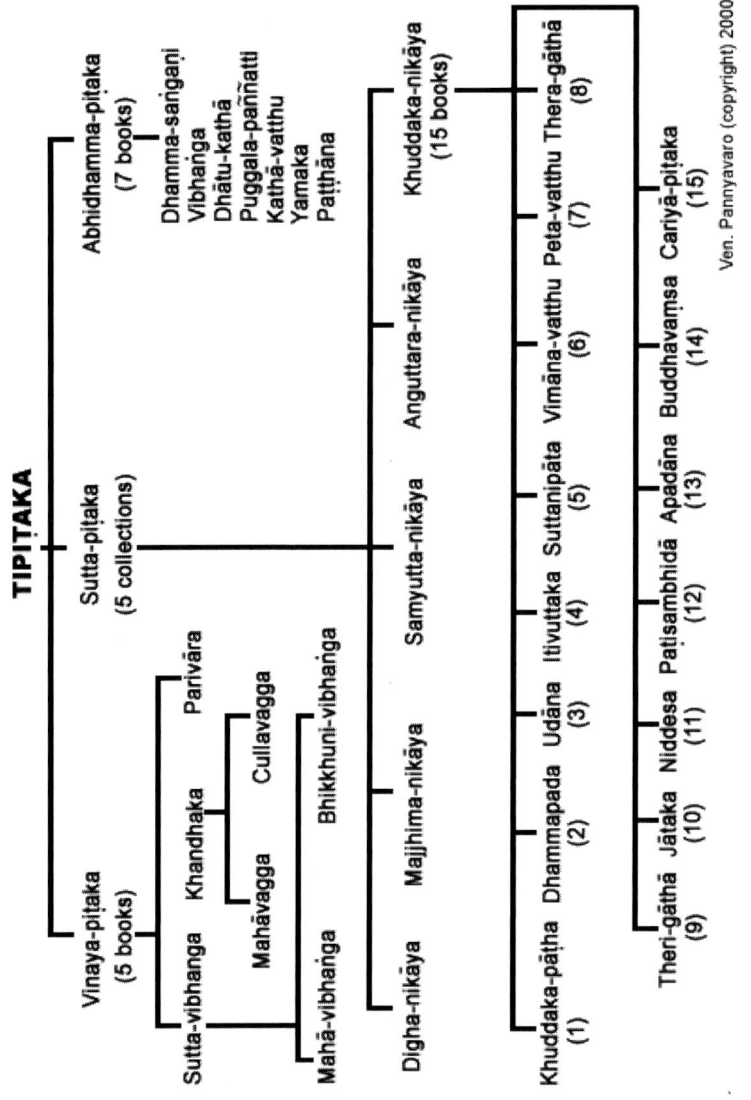

Figure 3. Outline of the *Tipiṭaka* (from www.buddhanet.net)

as a comprehensive description of Buddhist psychology. The *Abhidhamma* is considered to be derived from the *Sutta-piṭaka* and *Vinaya-piṭaka*. It is likely that it is a later addition to the *Pāli* Canon that was formulated by many Buddhist monks over several centuries. Different early Buddhist schools developed slightly different *Abhidhammas,* some of which exist today and are available for comparison. Another layer of *Pāli* writing added to the *Tipiṭaka* over time has been the *Pāli* Commentaries, which are explanations and elaborations on the *Sutta-piṭaka* and *Vinaya-piṭaka* which were developed and transmitted by the Buddha's disciples. The existing version of the commentaries was likely written down by the Indian monk Buddhagosa in Sri Lanka 1000 years after the Buddha's death. He also authored the *Visuddhimagga* (The Path of Purification) which is a detailed Buddhist practice manual that has become the *de facto* meditation guide for many modern *Theravāda* Buddhists.

Over time there has been much debate over the veracity of the *Pāli* Canon and in particular how much of the meaning of what the Buddha really taught has been changed. As the Dharma has traversed the millennia from the mouth of the Buddha living in Ancient India to the written English translations we hold in our hands, we can imagine several ways in which the original teachings may have drifted from the Buddha's words (*Buddhavacana*):

- Misinterpretation of the words of the Buddha by one of the original disciples
- Drift in the meaning and precision of the Dharma as the oral transmission of the teachings went from one generation to the next
- Changes due to the shift from the original language the Buddha spoke to *Pāli*
- Intentional redaction by misguided monks
- Transcription errors in copying written texts
- Difficulties in translating ancient *Pāli* into modern-day English
- Differences in cultural context and human psychological makeup between the Buddha's time and ours
- Miscomprehension of the teachings by the practitioner or teachers

Given all these possible sources of error one can be left doubting the usefulness of *sutta* study. However, I believe that there is much to learn from the *suttas* even if we don't know how precisely they reproduce what the Buddha taught. As a starting place we see that much of what we read in one *sutta* is reflected accurately in other places of the Canon, sometimes in multiple contexts. Also, there has been much scholarship comparing *Pāli* texts to surviving early Buddhist texts from non-*Theravāda* schools that were originally written in Sanskrit or other ancient Asian languages. Comparing the *Pāli Tipiṭaka* to parallel sections of Chinese translations of early Sanskrit Buddhist texts (the *Āgamas*) has been particularly fruitful. There are a few interesting and significant variances. However, scholars have found good concordance with the majority of the sections compared in these two bodies of literature so far. The internal and external consistency of the Dharma coupled with its voluminous logical and skillful explication found in the *suttas* argues for its authenticity and utility in modern life.

In studying the *suttas* it is helpful to approach new material with an open mind, sometimes imagining oneself in the setting depicted in the *sutta*. As we can never know for sure if the existent texts are accurate renditions of what the Buddha actually taught, we need to have a sense of curiosity and investigation. During his time the Buddha himself recommended that one not blindly accept his or anyone's words, rather one should investigate them for oneself (with the aid of the wise). He particularly encouraged the practitioner to determine if putting into action the teachings would cause harm to oneself or others or if they might be beneficial. If one determines that harm would result from the practices proposed by the teachings, then they should be abandoned. If no harm will come from them, then they can be pursued and practiced:

Kalamas, don't go by reports, by legends, by traditions, by scripture, by logical conjecture, by inference, by analogies, by agreement through pondering views, by probability, or by the thought, 'This contemplative is our teacher.' When you know for yourselves that, 'These qualities are unskillful; these qualities are blameworthy; these qualities are criticized by the wise; these qualities, when adopted & carried out, lead to harm & to suffering' — then you should abandon them.

When you know for yourselves that, 'These qualities are skillful; these qualities are blameless; these qualities are praised by the wise; these qualities, when adopted & carried out, lead to welfare & to happiness' — then you should enter & remain in them.

- AN 3.65 The Kalama Sutta: To the Kalamas

The opposite extreme to blindly accepting all that one reads in the *suttas* is to view them as fiction, the mythical scriptures of a foreign religion, or as too archaic or esoteric to apply to our current situation. I propose a middle path of reading the *suttas* with discernment, reflecting on them over time, comparing them to what one has already accepted as true Dharma, incorporating the new information into one's understanding, meditating with it and then wisely putting into practice the new teachings. This work is best done with others, either wise friends (*kalyāṇa-mitta*) on the path of Dharma practice or a qualified teacher. There are also a great many books and internet resources available to aid the student of the *suttas*. Some of these are listed in the Reference section.

The Buddha

Truly seeing Dhamma, one sees me; seeing me one sees Dhamma.

- *SN 22.87 Vakkali Sutta: To Vakkali* (Translated by Walshe)

The early *Pāli* Canon records sparse biographical details about the early life of the Buddha before his enlightenment. In the texts the Buddha usually refers to himself as the *Tathāgata* which is literally translated as "the thus gone one" or "the thus come one," which may mean "one who has gone beyond the round of rebirths". This enigmatic appellate underlies the fact that the Buddha was not interested in creating a personality cult. His teaching mission was for the purpose of disseminating the Dharma and not about promoting himself as a legendary figure. Later additions to the *Pāli* Canon and the *Pāli* Commentaries give several versions of the Buddha's life. Some accounts are quite fantastical and incredible by modern logical sensibilities. A few modern authors have removed any mythical seeming or grandiose elements from the Buddha's life story to provide a secular rendition. What follows is an account that seeks to form a middle path and one which is accepted by many modern *Theravāda* Buddhists.

Legend has it that the current Buddha is but one in a long line of buddhas, each appearing at a time in this world when individuals are ripe to benefit from the Dharma and are willing and capable of practicing the teachings to their conclusion (*Nibbāna* - unbinding, awakening to freedom from suffering). According to this view, each Buddha does not develop unique teachings but rediscovers the same Dharma as his predecessors:

> It is just as if a man, traveling along a wilderness track, were to see an ancient path, an ancient road, traveled by people of former times. He would follow it. Following it, he would see an ancient city, an ancient capital inhabited by people of former times, complete with parks, groves, & ponds, walled, delightful. He would go to address the king or the king's minister, saying, 'Sire, you should know that while traveling along a wilderness track I saw an ancient path... I followed it... I saw an ancient city, an ancient capital... complete with parks, groves, & ponds, walled, delight-

ful. Sire, rebuild that city!' The king or king's minister would rebuild the city, so that at a later date the city would become powerful, rich, & well-populated, fully grown & prosperous.

In the same way I saw an ancient path, an ancient road, traveled by the Rightly Self-awakened Ones of former times. And what is that ancient path, that ancient road, traveled by the Rightly Self-awakened Ones of former times? Just this noble eightfold path: right view, right aspiration, right speech, right action, right livelihood, right effort, right mindfulness, right concentration. That is the ancient path, the ancient road, traveled by the Rightly Self-awakened Ones of former times. I followed that path. Following it, I came to direct knowledge of aging & death, direct knowledge of the origination of aging & death, direct knowledge of the cessation of aging & death, direct knowledge of the path leading to the cessation of aging & death.

- SN 12.65 The Nagara Sutta: The City

As this passage shows, the path that is discovered, the fundamental teaching of all buddhas, is the Noble Eight-fold Path (*ariya aṭṭhaṅgikamagga*), and by implication, the Four Noble Truths (*cattāri ariyasaccāni*). The Four Noble Truths are at the core of the Buddha's teachings and are found throughout the *suttas* (see below).

The Legend of the Buddha

Many eons ago the Buddha-to-be (called the "*Bodhisatta*", Sanskrit - *Bodhisattva*) was a wandering *Samaṇa* named Sumedo. He met the Buddha of the time, Dipankara, and was so awed by him that he vowed to delay his own awakening in order to become a Buddha himself. He spent many lifetimes being reborn as various beings: humans, animals, and gods. These stories are told in the *Jātaka* tales of the *Sutta-piṭaka.* In each life he expended considerable effort to develop the *pāramīs* (perfections), which are skillful ethical and spiritual qualities such as generosity, morality, renunciation, etc. In his last life he was born as Siddattha Gotama, the son of a chieftain of a small republic called Sakka, located at the base of the Himalayas. The capital of Sakka was Kapilavathu (see Figure 1).

The *Bodhisatta* was raised to follow in the footsteps of his father to become the next leader of his people. It is said that he was spoiled with all of the sensual gratification of nobility and sheltered from the reality of suffering in the world. All was well with this arrangement for many years. The *Bodhisatta* married and lived a life of privilege with his wife. Then, after the birth of his son when the *Bodhisatta* was 29 years old, he left his wife and child, the palace and province he was due to inherit. What inspired him to leave home and become a *Samaṇa* in search of spiritual truth was his contact with the four divine messengers: a sick person, an aging person, a dead body, and a *Samaṇa*. Having previously been sheltered from these sights by his father's control, the *Bodhisatta* saw for the first time the suffering that is inherent in life and a potential way out of it:

> I, too, monks, before my Awakening, when I was an unawakened bodhisatta, being subject myself to birth, sought what was likewise subject to birth. Being subject myself to aging… illness… death… sorrow… defilement, I sought [happiness in] what was likewise subject to illness… death… sorrow… defilement. The thought occurred to me, 'Why do I, being subject myself to birth, seek what is likewise subject to birth? Being subject myself to aging… illness… death… sorrow… defilement, why do I seek what is likewise subject to illness… death… sorrow… defilement? What if I, being subject myself to birth, seeing the drawbacks of birth, were to seek the unborn, unexcelled rest from the yoke: Unbinding [Nibbāna]? What if I, being subject myself to aging… illness… death… sorrow… defilement, seeing the drawbacks of

aging... illness... death... sorrow... defilement, were to seek the aging-less, illness-less, deathless, sorrow-less,, unexcelled rest from the yoke: Unbinding?'

So, at a later time, while still young, a black-haired young man endowed with the blessings of youth in the first stage of life — and while my parents, unwilling, were crying with tears streaming down their faces — I shaved off my hair & beard, put on the ochre robe and went forth from the home life into homelessness.

- MN26: *The Ariyapariyesana sutta: The Noble Search*

This account of the early life of the Buddha is considered by some to be mythical. Some believe that Siddatha Gotama did not spend many lives cultivating the *pāramīs* but was born into an ordinary single life and went on to become the Buddha by the power of his own mind. This view claims that the mythological elements of the Buddha's story were later embellishments from devout followers. The early texts do not have conclusive biographical information to clarify this controversy. There is scholarly debate on the legitimacy of the mystical elements of the *Pāli* Canon and how the teachings can be interpreted in our modern life (i.e. see Batchelor in the Reference section).

The Quest for Enlightenment

The *Bodhisatta* spent the next few years as a traveling *Samaṇa* in the Ganges River Basin searching for liberation. It was commonly accepted at the time that all beings possessed a soul that wandered from one life to the next in what was called *saṃsāra* – the wheel of suffering. *Samaṇas* such as the *Boddhisatta* were looking for a way to end this cycle of suffering by reaching liberation. Although many of his contemporaries claimed to have done this, the *Bodhisatta* was astute and saw no evidence that others had indeed ended permanently their suffering.

The *Boddhisatta* studied meditation techniques with several of the day's most renowned teachers. A passage from the *Majjhima Nikāya* indicates that he surpassed his teachers and was even offered the position of chief guru (see *MN* 26). He recognized that the refined meditative states (*jhānas* or meditative absorptions) would not in themselves lead to liberation and he declined the offer. He spent six years in ascetic practices leading a group of five other *Samaṇas*. Passages from the *suttas* describe in graphic detail the extreme measures the *Boddhisatta* took to torment his body and to tame his mind (i.e. MN 12). The belief behind these practices was that by torturing the body one could burn up one's negative *karma* and reach liberation from *saṃsāra*. There are still yogis in India today who believe this and practice extreme asceticism.

After years of trying such drastic practices as starvation, breath-holding, living like an animal, standing without sitting, always squatting, experiencing the extremes of weather, and pulling out his own hair, the *Bodhisatta* realized that all this effort was futile:

> I thought: 'Whatever priests or contemplatives in the past have felt painful, racking, piercing feelings due to their striving, this is the utmost. None have been greater than this. Whatever priests or contemplatives in the future will feel painful, racking, piercing feelings due to their striving, this is the utmost. None will be greater than this. Whatever priests or contemplatives in the present are feeling painful, racking, piercing feelings due to their striving, this is the utmost. None is greater than this. But with this racking practice of austerities I haven't attained any superior human state, any distinction in knowledge or vision worthy of the noble ones. Could there be another path to Awakening?'
>
> -MN36 *Maha-Saccaka Sutta: The Longer Discourse to Saccaka*

What follows is a famous account from the same *sutta* on how the Buddha achieved enlightenment. In this passage he realizes that with a neglected and weakened body he would not be able to develop the powers of mind needed for awakening. Although he had earlier rejected the *jhānas* as being states of awakening he discovered that they were essential to prepare the mind for the deep insights necessary to liberate the mind. After taking nourishment he sat down to meditate underneath a Pipal tree which later Buddhism was to celebrate and revere as the Bodhi Tree:

> I thought: 'I recall once, when my father the Sakyan was working, and I was sitting in the cool shade of a rose-apple tree, then — quite secluded from sensuality, secluded from unskillful mental qualities — I entered & remained in the first jhana: rapture & pleasure born from seclusion, accompanied by directed thought & evaluation. Could that be the path to Awakening?' Then following on that memory came the realization: 'That is the path to Awakening.' I thought: 'So why am I afraid of that pleasure that has nothing to do with sensuality, nothing to do with unskillful mental qualities?' I thought: 'I am no longer afraid of that pleasure that has nothing to do with sensuality, nothing to do with unskillful mental qualities, but that pleasure is not easy to achieve with a body so extremely emaciated. Suppose I were to take some solid

food: some rice & porridge.' So I took some solid food: some rice & porridge. Now five monks had been attending on me, thinking, 'If Gotama, our contemplative, achieves some higher state, he will tell us.' But when they saw me taking some solid food — some rice & porridge — they were disgusted and left me, thinking, 'Gotama the contemplative is living luxuriously. He has abandoned his exertion and is backsliding into abundance.'

So when I had taken solid food and regained strength, then — quite secluded from sensuality, secluded from unskillful mental qualities, I entered & remained in the first jhana: rapture & pleasure born from seclusion, accompanied by directed thought & evaluation. But the pleasant feeling that arose in this way did not invade my mind or remain. With the stilling of directed thoughts & evaluations, I entered & remained in the second jhana: rapture & pleasure born of concentration, unification of awareness free from directed thought & evaluation — internal assurance. But the pleasant feeling that arose in this way did not invade my mind or remain. With the fading of rapture I remained equanimous, mindful, & alert, and sensed pleasure with the body. I entered & remained in the third jhana, of which the noble ones declare, 'Equanimous & mindful, he has a pleasant abiding.' But the pleasant feeling that arose in this way did not invade my mind or remain. With the abandoning of pleasure & pain — as with the earlier disappearance of elation & distress — I entered & remained in the fourth jhana: purity of equanimity & mindfulness, neither pleasure nor pain. But the pleasant feeling that arose in this way did not invade my mind or remain.

Following this preparatory work the Buddha was ready to apply his concentrated mind toward insight into the nature of things as they actually are. Here he describes his first knowledge gained in the first watch of the night of his awakening:

When the mind was thus concentrated, purified, bright, unblemished, rid of defilement, pliant, malleable, steady, & attained to imperturbability, I directed it to the knowledge of recollecting my past lives. I recollected my manifold past lives, i.e., one birth, two...five, ten...fifty, a hundred, a thousand, a hundred thousand, many eons of cosmic contraction, many eons of cosmic expansion, many eons of cosmic contraction & expansion: 'There I had such a name, belonged to such a clan, had such an appearance. Such was my food, such my experience of pleasure & pain, such the end of my life. Passing away from that state, I re-arose there. There too I had such a name, belonged to such a clan, had such an appearance. Such was my food, such my experience of pleasure & pain, such the end of my life. Passing away from that state, I re-arose here.' Thus I remembered my manifold past lives in their modes & details.

The second knowledge gained in the second watch of the night:

When the mind was thus concentrated, purified, bright, unblemished, rid of defilement, pliant, malleable, steady, & attained to imperturbability, I directed it to the knowledge of the passing away & reappearance of beings. I saw — by means of the divine eye, purified & surpassing the human — beings passing away & re-appearing, and I discerned how they are inferior & superior, beautiful & ugly, fortunate & unfortunate in accordance with their kamma: 'These beings — who were endowed with bad conduct of body, speech, & mind, who reviled the noble ones, held wrong views and undertook actions under the influence of wrong views — with the break-up of the body, after death, have re-appeared in the plane of deprivation, the bad destination, the lower realms, in hell. But these beings — who were endowed with good conduct of body, speech & mind, who did not revile the noble ones, who held right views and undertook actions under the influence of right views — with the break-up of the body, after death, have re-appeared in the good destinations, in the heavenly world.' Thus — by means of the divine eye, purified & surpassing the human — I saw beings passing away & re-appearing, and I discerned how they are inferior & superior, beautiful & ugly, fortunate & unfortunate in accordance with their kamma.

The Buddha achieved the third and final knowledge in the third watch of the night which culminated in his awakening:

When the mind was thus concentrated, purified, bright, unblemished, rid of defilement, pliant, malleable, steady, & attained to imperturbability, I directed it to the knowledge of the ending of the mental fermentations. I discerned, as it was actually present, that 'This is stress... This is the origination of stress... This is the cessation of stress... This is the way leading to the cessation of stress... These are fermentations... This is the origination of fermentations... This is the cessation of fermentations... This is the way leading to the cessation of fermentations.' My heart, thus knowing, thus seeing, was released from the fermentation of sensuality, released from the fermentation of becoming, released from the fermentation of ignorance. With release, there was the knowledge, 'Released.'

I discerned that 'Birth is ended, the holy life fulfilled, the task done. There is nothing further for this world.'

- MN 36 Mahāsaccaka Sutta: The Longer Discourse to Saccaka

This describes the Buddha's realization of the Four Noble Truths. The *Theravāda* tradition considers that *Nibbāna* is the highest goal of practice and is not a mere intellectual grasp of the Four Noble Truths but a deep intuitive and integrated understanding of their full implications. It is a freedom from all greed, hatred and delusion; from all suffering. Legend has these as the first words the Buddha uttered after his awakening:

> Through many births
> I have wandered on and on,
> Searching for, but never finding,
> The builder of [this] house.
> To be born again and again is suffering.
> House-builder, you're seen!
> You will not build a house again!
> All the rafters are broken,
> The ridge pole destroyed,
> The mind, gone to the Unconstructed,
> has reached the end of craving!

-Dhp 153-154.

In reaching *Nibbāna* the Buddha became an *Arahat* (fully enlightened being). There are numerous *sutta* passages addressing the nature of *Arahatship*. Some similes are given such as the going out of a flame, the quenching of thirst for continued rebirth, and the highest bliss knowable. There is debate among scholars and practitioners as to whether *Nibbāna* is a transcendent state, a mental continuum, or an ideal way of living in this world. For the purposes of this introduction, we will leave the debate with this definition:

> The destruction of lust, hatred, and delusion is called Arahatship.
>
> - *SN 38.2 Jambukhadakasamyutta* (tr. Ven. Bodhi)

The Decision to Teach the Dharma

After achieving *Nibbāna* the Buddha, according to the Commentaries, spent several weeks at the same location (modern day Bodh Gaya). It is said that he meditated deeply on the human condition and developed a detailed understanding of the Dharma. Before embarking on his teaching ministry, he paused and considered not spreading the word of the Dharma:

Then the thought occurred to me, 'This Dhamma that I have attained is deep, hard to see, hard to realize, peaceful, refined, beyond the scope of conjecture, subtle, to-be-experienced by the wise. But this generation delights in attachment, is excited by attachment, enjoys attachment. For a generation delighting in attachment, excited by attachment, enjoying attachment, this/that conditionality & dependent co-arising are hard to see. This state, too, is hard to see: the resolution of all fabrications, the relinquishment of all acquisitions, the ending of craving; dispassion; cessation; Unbinding. And if I were to teach the Dhamma and others would not understand me, that would be tiresome for me, troublesome for me.'

Just then these verses, unspoken in the past, unheard before, occurred to me:

Enough now with teaching
    what
    only with difficulty
    I reached.
This Dhamma is not easily realized
by those overcome
with aversion & passion.

What is abstruse, subtle,
>   deep,
>   hard to see,
going against the flow —
those delighting in passion,
cloaked in the mass of darkness,
>   won't see.

"Then Brahma Sahampati [a god], having known with his own awareness the line of thinking in my awareness, thought: 'The world is lost! The world is destroyed! The mind of the Tathagata, the Arahant, the Rightly Self-awakened One inclines to dwelling at ease, not to teaching the Dhamma!' Then, just as a strong man might extend his flexed arm or flex his extended arm, Brahma Sahampati disappeared from the Brahma-world and reappeared in front of me. Arranging his upper robe over one shoulder, he knelt down with his right knee on the ground, saluted me with his hands before his heart, and said to me: 'Lord, let the Blessed One teach the Dhamma! Let the One-Well-Gone teach the Dhamma! There are beings with little dust in their eyes who are falling away because they do not hear the Dhamma. There will be those who will understand the Dhamma.'

Then, having understood Brahma's invitation, out of compassion for beings, I surveyed the world with the eye of an Awakened One. As I did so, I saw beings with little dust in their eyes and those with much, those with keen faculties and those with dull, those with good attributes and those with bad, those easy to teach and those hard, some of them seeing disgrace & danger in the other world. Just as in a pond of blue or red or white lotuses, some lotuses — born & growing in the water — might flourish while immersed in the water, without rising up from the water; some might stand at an even level with the water; while some might rise up from the water and stand without being smeared by the water — so too, surveying the world with the eye of an Awakened One, I saw beings with little dust in their eyes and those with much, those with keen faculties and those with dull, those with good attributes and those with bad, those easy to teach and those hard, some of them seeing disgrace & danger in the other world.

Having seen this, I answered Brahma Sahampati in verse:

Open are the doors to the Deathless
to those with ears.
Let them show their conviction.

> Perceiving trouble, O Brahma,
> I did not tell people
> > the refined,
> > sublime Dhamma.

- MN26: The Ariyapariyesana sutta: The Noble Search

With that legendary invitation from the highest deity of the *Brahmin*s, the Buddha decided to teach the Dharma. It seems unlikely that the Buddha, having spent lifetimes over the eons training to be a Buddha whose purpose it is to discover and teach the Dharma would hesitate at the very pinnacle of his efforts. However, this dramatic twist may have lent credibility to the Buddhist argument that their founder was superior to all other spiritual teachers and gods and that his Dharma is the most sublime. And what is the Dharma that he espoused?

The Dharma

After some deliberation over whom to teach the Dharma the Buddha decided to find his former group of five *Samaṇa* followers. He thought that of all the people he knew they might be ripe for the teachings. He traveled some distance on foot to find them. When they saw him coming, by mutual consent, they agreed to ignore the Buddha. As he came closer however, they observed that the Buddha had such an aura about him that they could not keep their pact to avoid him. Once he convinced them to listen, he gave his first discourse which set in motion the wheel of the Dharma and began his teaching mission.

The First Discourse

I have heard that on one occasion the Blessed One was staying at Varanasi in the Game Refuge at Isipatana. There he addressed the group of five monks:

[The middle way]

There are these two extremes that are not to be indulged in by one who has gone forth [*as a Samaṇa*]. Which two? That which is devoted to sensual pleasure with reference to sensual objects: base, vulgar, common, ignoble, unprofitable; and that which is devoted to self-affliction: painful, ignoble, unprofitable. Avoiding both of these extremes, the middle way realized by the Tathagata — producing vision, producing knowledge — leads to calm, to direct knowledge, to self-awakening, to Unbinding.

[The Noble Eightfold Path]

And what is the middle way realized by the Tathagata that — producing vision, producing knowledge — leads to calm, to direct knowledge, to self-awakening, to Unbinding? Precisely this Noble Eightfold Path: right view, right resolve, right speech, right action, right livelihood, right effort, right mindfulness, right concentration. This is the middle way realized by the Tathagata that — producing vision, producing knowledge — leads to calm, to direct knowledge, to self-awakening, to Unbinding.

[The Four Noble Truths]

Now this, monks, is the noble truth of stress: Birth is stressful, aging is stressful, death is stressful; sorrow, lamentation, pain, distress, & despair are stressful; association with the unbeloved is stressful, separation from the loved is stressful, not getting what is wanted is stressful. In short, the five clinging-aggregates are stressful.

And this, monks, is the noble truth of the origination of stress: the craving that makes for further becoming — accompanied by passion & delight, relishing now here & now there — i.e., craving for sensual pleasure, craving for becoming, craving for non-becoming.

And this, monks, is the noble truth of the cessation of stress: the remainderless fading & cessation, renunciation, relinquishment, release, & letting go of that very craving.

And this, monks, is the noble truth of the way of practice leading to the cessation of stress: precisely this Noble Eightfold Path — right view, right resolve, right speech, right action, right livelihood, right effort, right mindfulness, right concentration.

[The Four Tasks of The Four Noble Truths]

Vision arose, insight arose, discernment arose, knowledge arose, illumination arose within me with regard to things never heard before: 'This is the noble truth of stress.' Vision arose, insight arose, discernment arose, knowledge arose, illumination arose within me with regard to things never heard before: 'This noble truth of stress is to be comprehended.' Vision arose, insight arose, discernment arose, knowledge arose, illumination arose within me with regard to things never heard before:' This noble truth of stress has been comprehended.'

Vision arose, insight arose, discernment arose, knowledge arose, illumination arose within me with regard to things never heard before: 'This is the noble truth of the origination of stress'... 'This noble truth of the origination of stress is to be abandoned' ... 'This noble truth of the origination of stress has been abandoned.'

Vision arose, insight arose, discernment arose, knowledge arose, illumination arose within me with regard to things never heard before: 'This is the noble truth of the cessation of stress'... 'This noble truth of the cessation of stress is to be directly experienced'... 'This noble truth of the cessation of stress has been directly experienced.'

Vision arose, insight arose, discernment arose, knowledge arose, illumination arose within me with regard to things never heard before: 'This is the noble truth of the way of practice leading to the cessation of stress'... 'This noble truth of the way of practice leading to the cessation of stress is to be developed'... 'This noble truth of the way of practice leading to the cessation of stress has been developed.'

And, monks, as long as this — my three-round, twelve-permutation knowledge & vision concerning these four noble truths as they have come to be — was not pure, I did not claim to have directly awakened to the right self-awakening unexcelled in the cosmos with its deities, Maras, & Brahmas, with its contemplatives & priests, its royalty & commonfolk. But as soon as this — my three-round, twelve-permutation knowledge & vision concerning these four noble truths as they have come to be — was truly pure, then I did claim to have directly awakened to the right self-awakening unexcelled in the cosmos with its deities, Maras & Brahmas, with its contemplatives & priests, its royalty & commonfolk. Knowledge & vision arose in me: 'Unprovoked is my release. This is the last birth. There is now no further becoming.'"

That is what the Blessed One said. Gratified, the group of five monks delighted at his words. And while this explanation was being given, there arose to Ven. Kondañña the dustless, stainless Dhamma eye: Whatever is subject to origination is all subject to cessation.

And when the Blessed One had set the Wheel of Dhamma in motion, the earth devas cried out: "At Varanasi, in the Game Refuge at Isipatana, the Blessed One has set in motion the unexcelled Wheel of Dhamma that cannot be stopped by priest or contemplative, deva, Maraor God or anyone in the cosmos." On hearing the earth devas' cry, the devas of the Four Kings' Heaven took up the cry... the devas of the Thirty-three... the Yama devas... the Tusita devas... the Nimmanarati devas... the Paranimmitavasavatti devas... the devas of Brahma's retinue took up the cry: "At Varanasi, in the Game Refuge at Isipatana, the Blessed One has set in motion the unexcelled Wheel of Dhamma that cannot be stopped by priest or contemplative, deva, Mara, or God or anyone at all in the cosmos."

So in that moment, that instant, the cry shot right up to the Brahma worlds. And this ten-thousand fold cosmos shivered & quivered & quaked, while a great, measureless radiance appeared in the cosmos, surpassing the effulgence of the devas.

Then the Blessed One exclaimed: "So you really know, Kondañña? So you really know?" And that is how Ven. Kondañña acquired the name Añña-Kondañña — Kondañña who knows.

- SN 56.11 Dhammacakkappavattana Sutta: *Setting the Wheel of Dharma in Motion*

This important *sutta* introduces many essential aspects of the Dharma. Figure 4 shows the *Dhammacakka* (Wheel of the Dharma) which is a well-known symbol of Buddhism. The wheel has eight spokes which represents the Noble Eightfold Path. The *sutta* begins with a discussion of the middle way. The Dharma is often referred to as a middle path between the extremes of indulgence in sensual pleasure and self-denial/affliction. That is, a balance between these two extremes of human nature. The *sutta* goes on to define the middle way as the Noble Eightfold Path. The eight factors are defined in the *sutta* and are a blueprint for living a Dharma-centered life that leads one to awakening. They are also the

Figure 4. *Dhammacakka* – The Wheel of Dharma

fourth of the Four Noble Truths. As mentioned earlier in this booklet, the truths are the bedrock of the Dharma and there are many passages in the *suttas* that stress the centrality of the truths in the teaching. There are a range of questions the Buddha called "speculative views" that he refused to answer. These are mostly metaphysical questions: "Do I exist? Is there a soul? What happens after death? How was the universe created?" Over and over he advises his students to avoid these questions as they distract one from the ultimate goal of Dharma practice which is to realize *Nibbāna*:

[These questions are]... a thicket of views, a wilderness of views, a contortion of views, a writhing of views, a fetter of views. It is accompanied by suffering, distress, despair, & fever, and it does not lead to disenchantment, dispassion, cessation; to calm, direct knowledge, full Awakening, Unbinding.

-*MN72 Aggivacchagotta Sutta:* To Vacchagotta on Fire

Instead he recommended that one focus on what is essential for the goal of awakening. Repeatedly he returns to the central importance of the Four Noble Truths. This is abbreviated in the following passage as:

Both formerly and now, monks, I declare only *dukkha* and the cessation of *dukkha*.

-*MN22 Alagaddūpama Sutta:* The Water-Snake Simile

Another aspect of the Four Noble Truths detailed in the *Dhammacakkappavattana Sutta* is the fact that they are not theories for pondering but practices to be repeatedly developed and perfected to completion. The first truth of *dukkha* (stress, suffering, unsatisfactoriness) is to be seen at work in our lives and comprehended. The second truth of the cause of *dukkha* (which is craving) is to be let go of. The third truth of the cessation of *dukkha* is to be achieved and realized. The fourth truth of the path of practice leading to the cessation of *dukkha* (the Noble Eightfold Path) is to be continually cultivated. In the process of his awakening, the Buddha tells his five friends, he accomplished all four tasks and achieved that which had never been done before – *Nibbāna*.

The *Dhammacakkappavattana Sutta* given above is an entire *sutta* and demonstrates many features of a typical *sutta*: 1) The *sutta* begins with "I have heard that one occasion..." which is reported to be Ānanda's recollection of the Buddha's words. Rather than stating that the following is gospel or an inviolable truth, the statement is only that this is what I've heard; 2) next is some background information on where the discourse takes place and who was present; 3) the body of the *sutta* gives the main teachings. These take the form of a declaration of the Buddha (as in this case), a brief utterance, a debate or question and answer session, or the description of a location, dream, simile, historical event or location; 4) the end of the *sutta* contains the effect that it had on the audience. In this case the monks were gratified by the discourse, Kondañña attains stream entry, the Devas cried out and the Buddha acknowledges Kondañña's attainment.

The *Pāli* Commentaries report this as the first *sutta* spoken by the Buddha. However some scholars question this and consider that the *Pāli* used in the discourse seems to be a later version and that the themes discussed were not well developed by the Buddha until later in his teaching dispensation. Regardless of its exact origin this important *sutta* is well worth studying and meditating with.

The *Pāli* Commentaries also state that the *sutta* reports the birth of the *Saṅgha* and that Koṇḍañña, on listening to these words, attained the first stage of enlightenment, stream entry. The following is recorded as the second discourse given by the Buddha to his first five disciples.

The Second Discourse

I have heard that on one occasion the Blessed One was staying at Varanasi in the Game Refuge at Isipatana. There he addressed the group of five monks:

"Form, monks, is not self. If form were the self, this form would not lend itself to dis-ease. It would be possible [to say] with regard to form, 'Let this form be thus. Let this form not be thus.' But precisely because form is not self, form lends itself to dis-ease. And it is not possible [to say] with regard to form, 'Let this form be thus. Let this form not be thus.'

[Likewise for the four other aggregates: feeling, perception, mental fabrications, and consciousness.]

"What do you think, monks — Is form constant or inconstant?"

"Inconstant, lord."

"And is that which is inconstant easeful or stressful?"

"Stressful, lord."

"And is it fitting to regard what is inconstant, stressful, subject to change as: 'This is mine. This is my self. This is what I am'?"

"No, lord."

[Likewise for the four other aggregates: feeling, perception, mental fabrications, and consciousness.]

"Thus, monks, any form whatsoever that is past, future, or present; internal or external; blatant or subtle; common or sublime; far or near: every form is to be seen as it actually is with right discernment as: 'This is not mine. This is not my self. This is not what I am.'

[Likewise for the four other aggregates: feeling, perception, mental fabrications, and consciousness.]

"Seeing thus, the well-instructed disciple of the noble ones grows disenchanted with form, disenchanted with feeling, disenchanted with perception, disenchanted with fabrications, disenchanted with consciousness. Disenchanted, he becomes dispassionate. Through dispassion, he is fully released. With full release, there is the knowledge, 'Fully released.' He discerns that 'Birth is ended, the holy life fulfilled, the task done. There is nothing further for this world.'"

That is what the Blessed One said. Gratified, the group of five monks delighted at his words. And while this explanation was being given, the hearts of the group of five monks, through not clinging (not being sustained), were fully released from fermentation/effluents.

- *SN 22.59 Anatta-lakkhana Sutta: The Discourse on the Not-self Characteristic)*

At the culmination of this discourse, all five of the Buddha's followers became fully enlightened. Then there were six *Arahats* in the world. The *sutta* develops the essential Buddhist themes of the *pañcupadānakkhandhā* (the five aggregates of clinging) and the *tilakkhaṇa* (the three characteristics of existence). The five aggregates are the Buddha's classification of the human psychophysical nature and figure prominently throughout the *suttas* as a means of understanding, working with and abandoning the clinging that is at the root of suffering. The three characteristics are fundamental aspects of human existence that are not readily visible but nonetheless true: *anicca* (impermanence), *dukkha* (suffering), and *anattā* (not-self). As this *sutta* claims, all that we experience is unreliable and subject to change. Due to this we find it inherently unsatisfactory and cannot find any unchanging essence to anything. It is our ignorance of these realities that keep us in suffering. Insight into these characteristics is essential for liberation:

> All created things are impermanent;
> All created things are suffering;
> All things are not-self;
> Seeing this with insight,
> One becomes disenchanted with suffering.
> This is the path to purity.

-Dhp 277-279

The *Saṅgha*

After this initial conversion the Buddha taught others and the Dharma spread throughout the region. Between his enlightenment and his death the Buddha taught for 45 years. The *Saṅgha* grew and became a diverse and at times complex community of perhaps several thousand followers during his lifetime (millions or more throughout the history of Buddhism). The Buddha taught both monastics and lay followers and stated that both could become enlightened. He taught men and women. He led a peripatetic life, preferring to be outdoors, at times in secluded meditation, and not bound to any one location. The *suttas* give only sparse biographical information about this period of his life. He had many supporters including many of the rulers of the region and some wealthy citizens. For the most part he avoided becoming involved in politics, intervening only when the *Saṅgha* was in jeopardy, an individual or group could be instructed to awakening or bloodshed could be averted.

The Buddha was originally reluctant to allow women to ordain as monastics (*bhikkhunis* – nuns). He consented only after Ānanda (his cousin and personal attendant) intervened on behalf of the women wanting to ordain. Even then, for the nuns he applied several rules in addition to what the monks had to observe. Although some have interpreted this as misogyny on the part of the Buddha, it was a daring move to acknowledge women as spiritual seekers and capable of achieving the liberation. In ancient India allowing women to have equal spiritual status to men would have been radical and unpopular. The Buddha managed to successfully integrate women into the monastic society and this arrangement has survived in various forms for 2500 years. Scholars such as Ven. Bhikkhu Analayo have suggested through comparative studies of *Vinaya* passages relating to the creation of the *Bhikkhuni Saṅgha* that the Buddha was not misogynistic but later redactions of texts by misguided monks portrayed him as such. Although we may never know with certainty the Buddha's stance on women in the *Saṅgha*, the *Pāli* Canon records many important teachings by women. There is a section about *bhikkhunis* in the *Saṃyutta Nikāya*, the *Therigatha* of the *Khuddhaka Nikāya* is a collection of inspiring verses spoken by awakened women, and a profound discourse is given by a *bhikkhuni* to her former husband in *sutta* number 44 of the *Majjhima Nikāya*.

The *suttas* give a rich and diverse matrix of the Buddha's teachings. Many *suttas* portray him replying to some interlocutor in response to pointed questions both practical and spiritual. In his teachings he used many colorful similes that give interesting views of life during that time and clarify the meaning of his words. The Buddha taught the Dharma out of compassion for the world and not for self-seeking motives.

The Noble Eightfold Path

The Buddha recommended that both monastic and lay followers should practice the Noble Eightfold Path. The following passage gives the Buddha's summary of the path:

> I have heard that at one time the Blessed One was staying in Savatthi at Jeta's Grove, Anathapindika's monastery.
>
> There he addressed the monks, saying, "Monks."
> "Yes, lord," the monks responded to him.
>
> The Blessed One said, "I will teach & analyze for you the Noble Eightfold Path. Listen & pay close attention. I will speak."
> "As you say, lord," the monks responded to him.

The Blessed One said, "Now what, monks, is the Noble Eightfold Path? Right view, right resolve, right speech, right action, right livelihood, right effort, right mindfulness, right concentration.

"And what, monks, is right view? Knowledge with regard to stress, knowledge with regard to the origination of stress, knowledge with regard to the stopping of stress, knowledge with regard to the way of practice leading to the stopping of stress: This, monks, is called right view.

"And what is right resolve? Being resolved on renunciation, on freedom from ill will, on harmlessness: This is called right resolve.

"And what is right speech? Abstaining from lying, abstaining from divisive speech, abstaining from abusive speech, abstaining from idle chatter: This, monks, is called right speech.

"And what, monks, is right action? Abstaining from taking life, abstaining from stealing, abstaining from unchastity: This, monks, is called right action.

"And what, monks, is right livelihood? There is the case where a disciple of the noble ones, having abandoned dishonest livelihood, keeps his life going with right livelihood: This, monks, is called right livelihood.

"And what, monks, is right effort? (**i**) There is the case where a monk generates desire, endeavors, activates persistence, upholds & exerts his intent for the sake of the non-arising of evil, unskillful qualities that have not yet arisen. (**ii**) He generates desire, endeavors, activates persistence, upholds & exerts his intent for the sake of the abandonment of evil, unskillful qualities that have arisen. (**iii**) He generates desire, endeavors, activates persistence, upholds & exerts his intent for the sake of the arising of skillful qualities that have not yet arisen. (**iv**) He generates desire, endeavors, activates persistence, upholds & exerts his intent for the maintenance, non-confusion, increase, plenitude, development, & culmination of skillful qualities that have arisen: This, monks, is called right effort.

"And what, monks, is right mindfulness? (**i**) There is the case where a monk remains focused on the body in & of itself — ardent, aware, & mindful — putting away greed & distress with reference to the world. (**ii**) He remains focused on feelings in & of themselves — ardent, aware, &

mindful — putting away greed & distress with reference to the world. (**iii**) He remains focused on the mind in & of itself — ardent, aware, & mindful — putting away greed & distress with reference to the world. (**iv**) He remains focused on mental qualities in & of themselves — ardent, aware, & mindful — putting away greed & distress with reference to the world. This, monks, is called right mindfulness.

"And what, monks, is right concentration? (**i**) There is the case where a monk — quite withdrawn from sensuality, withdrawn from unskillful (mental) qualities — enters & remains in the first jhana: rapture & pleasure born from withdrawal, accompanied by directed thought & evaluation. (**ii**) With the stilling of directed thoughts & evaluations, he enters & remains in the second jhana: rapture & pleasure born of concentration, unification of awareness free from directed thought & evaluation — internal assurance. (**iii**) With the fading of rapture, he remains equanimous, mindful, & alert, and senses pleasure with the body. He enters & remains in the third jhana, of which the Noble Ones declare, 'Equanimous & mindful, he has a pleasant abiding.' (**iv**) With the abandoning of pleasure & pain — as with the earlier disappearance of elation & distress — he enters & remains in the fourth jhana: purity of equanimity

& mindfulness, neither pleasure nor pain. This, monks, is called right concentration."

That is what the Blessed One said. Gratified, the monks delighted at his words.

- *SN 45.8 Maggavibhaṅga Sutta:* An Analysis of the Path

Other Important Teachings

To those new to the Dharma the Buddha usually recommended starting practice with *dāna* (giving) and *sīla* (ethical conduct). The development of these two qualities is the foundation upon which can be built a purified mind capable of insights that lead to mature Dharma practice and awakening.

If beings knew, as I know, the results of giving & sharing, they would not eat without having given, nor would the stain of selfishness overcome their minds. Even if it were their last bite, their last mouthful, they would not eat without having shared, if there were someone to receive their gift. But because beings do not know, as I know, the results of giving & sharing, they eat without having given. The stain of selfishness overcomes their minds.

- Iti 1.26

The Buddha taught that there are 10 skillful actions of body, speech, and mind that one should do while refraining from their opposites:

> And what is skillful? Abstaining from taking life is skillful, abstaining from taking what is not given... from sexual misconduct... from lying... from abusive speech... from divisive tale-bearing... abstaining from idle chatter is skillful. Lack of covetousness... lack of ill will... right views are skillful. These things are termed skillful.
>
> -MN 9 *Sammādiṭṭhi Sutta:* The Discourse on Right View

Karma and Rebirth

The *suttas* contain many passages regarding karma and rebirth. At the time of the Buddha these were widely accepted truths of the nature of existence:

> From an inconstruable beginning comes transmigration. A beginning point is not evident, though beings hindered by ignorance and fettered by craving are transmigrating & wandering on. What do you think, monks: Which is greater, the tears you have shed while transmigrating & wan-

dering this long, long time — crying & weeping from being joined with what is displeasing, being separated from what is pleasing — or the water in the four great oceans?"

This is the greater: the tears you have shed while transmigrating & wandering this long, long time — crying & weeping from being joined with what is displeasing, being separated from what is pleasing — not the water in the four great oceans.

- SN 15.1 *The Assu Sutta:* Tears

In our modern times many practitioners have difficulty accepting karma and rebirth, even though they may diligently engage other aspects of the Buddha's teachings. As karma and rebirth are difficult to experience directly, the controversy is understandable. Some scholars posit that the Buddha was only using these principles in his teachings because they were conventions of the times and to refute them openly would have been heresy, harmful, and would have derailed his teaching mission. Others argue that he was speaking metaphorically or that karma and rebirth teachings only apply to our momentary experience. That is that we are reborn into each new moment based on our past actions. Knowing how he placed truth above all, it is difficult to fully embrace those contemporary views that are opposed to a literal interpretation of the Canonical teachings on karma and rebirth. Over and over in the *suttas* we see discussions on karma and rebirth. In fact in several passages belief in them is considered the essence of Right View. Each student of the *suttas* will have to formulate his or her own working understanding on the subject.

There is a middle path between rejecting outright the principles of karma and rebirth and accepting them on blind faith. One can remain with an open mind toward these and other complicated or confusing teachings, while practicing the parts of the Dharma that one knows or can experience directly. Regarding karma, the Buddha taught that the most important thing in Dharma practice is to have skillful intentions:

> Intention, I tell you, is kamma. Intending, one does kamma by way of body, speech, and mind.
>
> - AN 6.63 *Nibbedhika Sutta:* Penetrative Sutta

If we proceed through life without setting skillful intentions we will be at the whim of the many unskillful habits of mind. These impediments to liberation and are what the Buddha described as the three unskillful root defilements [*mūla-kilesa*] or underlying tendencies of the mind [*anusaya*]: greed, hatred, and delusion. Dharma practice is a means to cleanse the mind of these tendencies and to avoid mental, verbal, or bodily actions based on them.

Three qualities of the world, great king, when arising, arise for harm, stress, & discomfort. Which three? Greed [as well as Aversion and Delusion], great king, is a quality of the world that, when arising, arises for harm, stress, & discomfort.

- SN 3.23 Loka sutta: The world discourse

The Four Establishments of Mindfulness

The most complete and extensive meditation instructions in the Pāli Canon are arguably those of the Satipaṭṭhāna Sutta (Four Establishments or Foundations of Mindfulness). There are two complete Satipaṭṭhāna Suttas found in the Pāli Canon and many other shorter versions and teachings involving satipaṭṭhāna. A summary of the four from the Satipaṭṭhāna Sutta is:

> This is the direct path for the purification of beings, for the overcoming of sorrow & lamentation, for the disappearance of pain & distress, for the attainment of the right method, & for the realization of Unbinding — in other words, the four frames of reference. Which four?

There is the case where a monk remains focused on the **body** in & of itself — ardent, alert, & mindful — putting aside greed & distress with reference to the world. He remains focused on **feelings… mind… mental qualities** in & of themselves — ardent, alert, & mindful — putting aside greed & distress with reference to the world.

- MN 10 *Satipaṭṭhāna Sutta*: The Four Establishments of Mindfulness (**Bold** markings added to highlight the four)

The *sutta* goes on to list over 20 different meditation objects and practices – all of which are contained within the four establishments: the body, feelings, mind states and *dhammas* (translated here as mental qualities, in other translations they are called phenomenon or categories of experience). Mindfulness of these objects is framed with attention to not clinging to them and with awareness of both one's own experience and that of others. This important *sutta* is well worth studying and practicing with. It has become the *de facto* meditation primer of the modern *Vipassanā* (Insight Meditation) movement. Scholars such as Ven. Analyo have performed comparative studies of the *Pāli Satipaṭṭhāna Sutta* and other versions. They speculate that the version present today is a compilation of several teachings of the Buddha that were arranged by later Buddhists and meant to be a comprehensive set of mindfulness instructions for meditators to follow.

Dependent Origination

Another key teaching of the Buddha is dependent origination or dependent co-arising (*paṭicca samuppāda*). The following well known passage is from the Buddha indicating the importance of dependent origination:

> Whoever sees dependent co-arising sees the Dhamma; whoever sees the Dhamma sees dependent co-arising.
>
> - MN 28 *Mahāhatthipadopama Sutta:* The Great Elephant Footprint Simile

The Buddha lists the 12 links of dependent origination in the following *sutta*:

> Dwelling at Savatthi... "Monks, I will describe & analyze dependent co-arising for you.
>
> "And what is dependent co-arising? From ignorance as a requisite condition come fabrications. From fabrications as a requisite condition comes consciousness. From con-

sciousness as a requisite condition comes name-&-form. From name-&-form as a requisite condition come the six sense media. From the six sense media as a requisite condition comes contact. From contact as a requisite condition comes feeling. From feeling as a requisite condition comes craving. From craving as a requisite condition comes clinging/sustenance. From clinging/sustenance as a requisite condition comes becoming. From becoming as a requisite condition comes birth. From birth as a requisite condition, then aging & death, sorrow, lamentation, pain, distress, & despair come into play. Such is the origination of this entire mass of stress & suffering.

"Now what is *aging and death?* Whatever aging, decrepitude, brokenness, graying, wrinkling, decline of life-force, weakening of the faculties of the various beings in this or that group of beings, that is called aging. Whatever deceasing, passing away, breaking up, disappearance, dying, death, completion of time, break up of the aggregates, casting off of the body, interruption in the life faculty of the various beings in this or that group of beings, that is called death.

"And what is *birth?* Whatever birth, taking birth, descent, coming-to-be, coming-forth, appearance of aggregates, &

acquisition of [sense] media of the various beings in this or that group of beings, that is called birth.

"And what is *becoming?* These three are becomings: sensual becoming, form becoming, & formless becoming. This is called becoming.

"And what is *clinging/sustenance?* These four are clingings: sensuality clinging, view clinging, precept & practice clinging, and doctrine of self clinging. This is called clinging.

"And what is *craving?* These six are classes of craving: craving for forms, craving for sounds, craving for smells, craving for tastes, craving for tactile sensations, craving for ideas. This is called craving.

"And what is *feeling?* These six are classes of feeling: feeling born from eye-contact, feeling born from ear-contact, feeling born from nose-contact, feeling born from tongue-contact, feeling born from body-contact, feeling born from intellect-contact. This is called feeling.

"And what is *contact?* These six are classes of contact: eye-contact, ear-contact, nose-contact, tongue-contact, body-contact, intellect-contact. This is called contact.

"And what are *the six sense media?* These six are sense media: the eye-medium, the ear-medium, the nose-medium, the tongue-medium, the body-medium, the intellect-medium. These are called the six sense media.

"And what is *name-&-form?* Feeling, perception, intention, contact, & attention: This is called name. The four great elements, and the form dependent on the four great elements: This is called form. This name & this form are called name-&-form.

"And what is *consciousness?* These six are classes of consciousness: eye-consciousness, ear-consciousness, nose-consciousness, tongue-consciousness, body-consciousness, intellect-consciousness. This is called consciousness.

"And what are *fabrications?* These three are fabrications: bodily fabrications, verbal fabrications, mental fabrications. These are called fabrications.

"And what is *ignorance?* Not knowing stress, not knowing the origination of stress, not knowing the cessation of stress, not knowing the way of practice leading to the cessation of stress: This is called ignorance.

"Now from the remainderless fading & cessation of that very ignorance comes the cessation of fabrications. From the cessation of fabrications comes the cessation of consciousness. From the cessation of consciousness comes the cessation of name-&-form. From the cessation of name-&-form comes the cessation of the six sense media. From the cessation of the six sense media comes the cessation of contact. From the cessation of contact comes the cessation of feeling. From the cessation of feeling comes the cessation of craving. From the cessation of craving comes the cessation of clinging/sustenance. From the cessation of clinging/sustenance comes the cessation of becoming. From the cessation of becoming comes the cessation of birth. From the cessation of birth, then aging & death, sorrow, lamentation, pain, distress, & despair all cease. Such is the cessation of this entire mass of stress & suffering."

- *SN 12.2 Paṭiccasamuppāda Vibhaṅga sutta:* Analysis of Dependent Origination

From this we see that suffering has causes and conditions and does not arise spontaneously and independently. Also, inherent in the cycle of dependent is the possibility of the cessation of suffering. This can be accomplished by interfering with or removing one or more of the links. However, the process of dependent origination is complex and dynamic and does not always occur in a linear progression. The 12 different links in the causal chain feedback upon and interact with each other. The process usually happens very rapidly and below the level or our ordinary awareness.

> Deep is this dependent co-arising, and deep its appearance. It's because of not understanding and not penetrating this Dhamma that this generation is like a tangled skein, a knotted ball of string, like matted rushes and reeds, and does not go beyond transmigration, beyond the planes of deprivation, woe, and bad destinations.
>
> - *DN 15.1 Mahānidāna Sutta:* The Great Causes Discourse

There are many other teachings of the Buddha found in the *suttas* that are considered by many to be essential. I refer the reader to the references for more in depth coverage of the Dharma.

The Buddha's Death

At the age of 80, after a rich and productive 40-year teaching career, the Buddha passed away. He left the *Saṅgha* to carry on the practice and teaching of the Dharma. *Sutta* number 16 of the *Digha Nikāya* (the *Mahāparinibbāna sutta*) describes the last year of the Buddha's life. Towards the end of his days we get a picture of an aging Buddha who's *Saṅgha* has grown large, diverse, and at times unruly. He has thwarted a plot to take his life and usurp control of the *Saṅgha* by his cousin Devadatta. His two main disciples, Sariputa and Mahamogollana have both already died. The two kings (Pasenadi and Bimbasara) who supported him for many years also had succumbed to treachery and death. The Buddha describes himself as old and worn out:

> Ananda, I am now old, worn out, venerable, one who has traversed life's path, I have reached the term of life which is eighty. Just as an old cart is made to go by being held together with straps, so the Tathāgata's body is kept going by being strapped up.
>
> -DN 16 *Mahāparinibbāna sutta:* The Great Passing Discourse (tr, Walshe)

Legend has it that the Buddha had knowledge of his impending death. He spent his last year wandering the region where he had spread the Dharma for many years. During this time he addressed his many followers giving his last teachings.

> Therefore, Ananda you should live as islands unto yourselves, being your own refuge with no one else as your refuge, with the Dhamma as an island, with the Dhamma as your refuge, with no other refuge. How does one do that? [With the four foundations of mindfulness.]
>
> - DN 16 *Mahāparinibbāna sutta:* The Great Passing Discourse (tr, Walshe)

When asked about the governance of the *Saṅgha* and a possible successor, the Buddha replied that the Dharma and discipline (*Vinaya*) should guide the *Saṅgha*. He did not want any one person to become the leader of the *Saṅgha*.

> [From his deathbed]... the Buddha said to Ananda: "... it may be that you will think: 'The Teacher's instruction has ceased, now we have no teacher!' It should not be seen like this, Ananda, for what I have taught and explained to you as Dhamma and Discipline will, at my passing, be your teacher.

- *DN 16 Mahāparinibbāna sutta:* The Great Passing Discourse (tr, Walshe)

The *sutta* records the Buddha's cause of death to be accidental food poisoning. His final words before reaching *parinibbāna* (complete unbinding, final *Nibbāna*) were:

Now, monks, I declare to you: All conditioned things are of the nature to decay – strive on untiringly.

- *DN 16 Mahāparinibbāna sutta:* The Great Passing Discourse (tr, Walshe)

Conclusion

After the Buddha's death many of his senior disciples met, discussed his teachings, and agreed upon the content and accuracy of their recall of his words. The result of this First Council of *Arahats* was to codify the Dharma and to establish a system of memorizing and orally reciting the teachings. These teachings have been handed down to us through the ages. Now we are left with a body of work that is rich, complex, at times confusing, and even occasionally self-contradictory. From the pages of that work we get a view of the man who awoke to the truth of suffering and discovered the path that leads to the end of suffering. Out of his compassion for the vast amount of pain and distress in the world he went on to become one of the greatest teachers known to this world. Today, from studying the *suttas* and practicing the Dharma, we can still benefit from the Buddha's words and discover our own path to *Nibbāna*:

> Its up to you to make strong effort;
> *Thatāgatas* merely tell you how.
> Following the path, those absorbed in meditation
> Will be freed from Māra's bonds.

-Dhp 276

This concludes our brief survey of *sutta* study. My hope is that this work has been helpful in giving an overview of the Buddha's teachings as portrayed in the *Pāli* Canon and that the information gained from it can be put to use toward the liberation of all beings. *Sutta* study combined with wise reflection and meditation practice provides a powerful platform for the transformation of suffering and awakening to freedom. If this subject has been of interest for you, there are numerous sources available these days for additional study-practice. Several works are recommended in the Reference section. A good starting place for self-study of the suttas is Bhikkhu Bodhi's book *In the Buddha's Words* or Glenn Wallis's *Basic Teachings of the Buddha*. Also, John Bullitt's essay *Befriending the Suttas* available on the Access to Insight Website is highly recommended.

We end with one of the most beloved and often recited *suttas* of the whole *Tipiṭaka, The Karaṇīya Metta Sutta* (The Sutta on Loving-kindness). This *sutta* gives both an ideal practice to emulate and an overview of the range of wholesome practices described in the Dharma:

The Karaṇīya Metta *Sutta*

To reach the state of peace
One skilled in the good
Should be
Capable and upright,
Straightforward and easy to speak to,
Gentle and not proud,
Contented and easily supported,
Living lightly and with few duties,
Wise and with senses calmed,
Not arrogant and without greed for supporters,
And should not do the least thing that the wise would criticize.
[One should reflect:]
"May all be happy and secure;
May all beings be happy at heart.
All living beings, whether weak or strong,
Tall, large, medium, or short,
Tiny or big,
Seen or unseen,
Near or distant,
Born or to be born,

May they all be happy.
Let no one deceive another
Or despise anyone anywhere;
Let no one through anger or aversion
Wish for others to suffer."
As a mother would risk her own life
To protect her child, her only child,
So toward all beings should one
Cultivate a boundless heart.
With loving-kindness for the whole world should one
Cultivate a boundless heart,
Above, below, and all around
Without obstruction, without hate and without ill-will.
Standing or walking, sitting or lying down,
Whenever one is awake,
May one stay with this recollection.
This is called a sublime abiding, here and now.
One who is virtuous, endowed with vision,
Not taken by views,
And having overcome all greed for sensual pleasure
Will not be reborn again.

Sn 1.8 The Karaṇīya Metta Sutta (translated by Gil Fronsdal)

Abbreviations

DN – *Digha Nikāya*

Dhp – *Dhammapada*

Iti - *Itivuttaka*

MN – *Majjhima Nikāya*

Sn – *Sutta Nipata*

SN – *Saṃyutta Nikāya*

AN – *Aṅguttara Nikāya*

Pāli Glossary

Āgamas – Early Buddhist scriptures existent in *Pāli*, Sanskrit or other languages.

Arahat – A fully enlightened being, one who has reached *Nibbāna*.

Bhikkhunis – Buddhist nuns.

Bhikkhus – Buddhist monks.

Boddhisatta – (*Bodhisattva* in Sanskrit) The name the Buddha called himself before his enlightenment. According to legend a *Boddhisatta* intentionally delays his enlightenment to cultivate the skills necessary to become a Buddha.

Brahmin – The highest class of the ancient Indian social class system, responsible for the performance of religious rituals.

Brahmā – *Brahmin* or Buddhist deity.

Dāna – giving, generosity. The preliminary step of practice.

Dharma – (*Dhamma* in *Pāli*) the teachings of the Buddha.

Dukkha – Suffering, stress, unsatisfactoriness.

Kamma – (karma in Sanskrit) Intention, volitional action. Skillful intention leads to happiness, unskillful intention leads to suffering.

Māra – An anthropomorphic representation of the defilements of the mind.

Nibbāna – (nirvana in Sanskrit) Enlightenment, awakening. the deathless, unbinding, cessation of suffering and the round of rebirths; The extinguishment of greed, hatred, and delusion.

Pañcupadānakkhandhā – the five aggregates of clinging: form, feeling, perception, mental formations, and consciousness. The Buddhist mental-physical classification of the human being.

Paṭicca samuppāda – dependent origination. A central teaching of the Dharma dealing with the conditional relationship of experience that leads to suffering.

Samaṇa – A wandering renunciant in search of spiritual truth.

Saṃsāra – The cycle of suffering and rebirths.

Saṅgha – Community of Buddhist practitioners, originally meant the ordained monastic community or community of enlightened ones.

Sīla - ethical conduct, an essential aspect of the Dharma and the foundational practice of Buddhism.

Tathāgata – the name the Buddha called himself, meaning "The thus gone one" or "The thus come one." Awakened one.

Tilakkhaṇa – The three marks or characteristics of existence: *anicca* (impermanence), *dukkha* (suffering), and *anattā* (not-self).

Tipiṭaka – The "Three Baskets" of teachings: the *Vinaya-piṭaka*, the *Sutta-piṭaka*, and the *Abhidhamma-piṭaka*; the *Pāli* Canon.

Theravāda - The only remaining early Buddhist school, the Southern School of Buddhism still in existence in Sri Lanka and Southeast Asia which considers the *Tipiṭaka* as its canon.

Acknowledgements

Many people have contributed to the making of this booklet. I am grateful for the years of support I have received from my teachers, in particular Gil Fronsdal, John Travis, Dennis Warren, Richard Shankman, Andrew Olendzki, Andrea Fella and Leigh Brasington. The support and kindness that I have received from the Sati Center for Buddhist Studies, the Insight Meditation Center and the Sacramento Insight Meditation *Saṅgha*s has been invaluable to my study, meditation and teaching practices. I am indebted to my many fellow students who toil to learn and practice the Dharma and who share their wisdom with me. I thank Tony Bernhard for his editorial assistance. I am also grateful to my loving wife, Jenny Mueller, our two cats and both of our families. My gratitude to the Buddha and the generations of his followers who have carried the Dharma through the ages and who have shown us the way to freedom is beyond words. May we practice their teachings diligently in order to reach the end of suffering.

References

Websites:

Translations, study guides, essays and audio talks by Ven. Thanissaro Bhikkhu found on the website: www.dhammatalks.org.

Access to Insight website: This is an excellent website that has much useful information for *sutta* study: www.accesstoinsight.org/.

The Sati Center for Buddhist Studies website has many articles and audio files on *sutta* studies: www.sati.org.

Sutta translations by Gil Fronsdal found at: www.insightmeditationcenter.org

Metta *sutta* self-guided study materials and many other *sutta* materials on the Barre Center for Buddhist Studies website: www.dharma.org/bcbs

Piya Tan's *sutta* study guides and translations:

www.dharmafarer.org

Books:

Analayo, Bhikkhu. 2003. *Satipaṭṭhānathana: the direct path to realization.* Windhorse Publications.

Batchelor, Stephen, 2010. *Confession of a Buddhist Atheist*, Spiegal and Grau.

Bodhi, Bhikkhu, (ed.) 2005. *In the Buddha's Words: An Anthology of Discourses from the Pāli Canon,* Wisdom Publications.

Bodhi, Bhikkhu, (tr.) 2012. *The Numerical Discourses of the Buddha: A Translation of the Anguttara Nikaya,* Wisdom Books, in press.

Bodhi, Bhikkhu. (ed.) 2000. *Abhidhammattha Sangaha: A comprehensive manual of Abhidhamma.* BPS Pariyatti Editions.

Fronsdal, Gil, (ed.) 2005, *The Dhammapada*, Shambala Press.

Harvey, Peter 2012. *An Introduction to Buddhism*, Second Edition, Cambridge University Press.

Murcott, Susan, 2006, First Buddhist Women: Poems and Stories of Awakening, Parallax Press.

Nanamoli, Bhikkhu and Bodhi, Bhikkhu, (tr.) 1995. *The Middle Length Discourses of the Buddha: A translation of the Majjhima Nikaya*, Wisdom Books.

Ñāṇamoli, Bhikkhu, ed. 1964. *The Life of the Buddha According to the Pāli Canon*, The Buddhist Publication Society.

Ñāṇamoli, Bhikkhu. (tr.) 1991. *The Path of Purification (Visuddhimagga)*. BPS.

Wallis, Glenn, 2007, *Basic Teachings of the Buddha*. Modern Library.

Walshe, Maurice, (tr.) 1987. *The Long Discourses of the Buddha: A translation of the Digha Nikaya*, Wisdom Books.

Audio:

Sutta study audio files by Ven. Bhikkhu Bodhi:
bodhimonastery.org
www.noblepath.org

An excellent series of talks by Stephen Batchelor on *The Life And Death Of Siddhattha Gotama*, www.dharmaseed.org.

The Sati Center for Buddhist Studies website has many audio and written files on *sutta* studies by numerous authors at www.sati.org.

Ven. Bhikkhu Analayo's *Madhyama Āgama* comparative study course: www.buddhismuskunde.uni-hamburg.de/fileadmin/pdf/analayo/lectures.htm

Sutta study talks by Ajahn Brahm, Ven. Bhikkhu Sujato and others: www.dhammanet.org

Audio files and writings on sutta studies by the author of this booklet: www.sactoinsight.org

Made in United States
North Haven, CT
11 January 2023